Be Successful By

The Easy Path to Your First Million

(It's Not Difficult to Get Rich)

Contents

An Exciting Journey to Your Goal

Many people complain about their economy. Some people confess they lack knowledge and competence, and they avoid taking full responsibility for their own economic conditions. Instead, they trust the so-called experts to take care of their economy.

What if they change focus and start dreaming? What if money is no problem? Then, they can do whatever they want. The passion starts to come together with goal setting and vision.

The conclusion is that most people are interested in their own economy only if they understand the link between a well-designed economy and how it gives them access to their own time. When they see how the private economy grows, things will become more and more exciting for them.

The secret is to save money, learn how to invest it, and make it work for you. Continue to save money on a regular basis, and your colleague, The Money Machine, will assist you in making it grow bigger and bigger.

To invest is to buy assets. An asset is something that puts more money into your pocket. The opposite is something that takes money from your pocket, for example, credits, a private house, etc. These are not assets. You need to have the definition clear when investing. You need to know what's an asset and what's not.

You need to learn how to invest, practice what you learn, sometimes fail, and get feedback from your results. Find out what works for you and get more and more skilled over time.

Do you feel you are selling your time to somebody just because you need the money? Do you want to spend your time doing something else but can't due to lack of money? Then, you need to take better control of your economy and your income streams. You need to build up a Money Machine.

The Right Attitude

"Without enthusiasm then what we have surrounded ourselves with becomes worthless."

— Stephen Richards

Attitude is everything! It is how you present yourself to the world and the people around you that truly show them what you are all about. Presentation is crucial. You can't just wish for yourself to become a millionaire and wake up to a stack of cash. It is a long process, which requires patience, hard work, and optimism.

Before you begin to think about how you'd want to deal with money, you must redirect your thought patterns. For instance, if you have self-deprecating thoughts about yourself such as "I will never amount to anything" or "I won't be able to pull it off." It is only going to hold you back. People tend to ignore their subconscious thoughts, but they don't realize that our subconscious thoughts drive our emotions. They are responsible for the things we do. When we think about negative things, knowingly or unknowingly, we end up doing something negative.

Think of it as a self-fulfilling prophecy. Or better yet, think of your mind as a child. If you constantly tell your child that they will never be able to climb a tree, they might never even try. Why? Because of the fear and negativity instilled in them by you. They will assume that the reason you think they won't be able to climb the tree is that a) they don't possess the means or resources to climb it, or b) they don't have it in them. In both cases, the child will hold back from taking chances. They will believe the limiting things you tell them. Similarly, if you keep telling your mind that you won't be successful or become a millionaire, your mind will take a back-seat. It will make you think, "Oh, yeah! I remember that I can't do a certain thing. So, why should I try in the first place?"

After you are done with curbing the negative thoughts, you can begin working towards your first million dollars.

To start the journey to your first million, you need to have the right attitude towards money, especially when it comes to obtaining obstacles. The first thing you have to do is to analyze yourself and your financial situation. Are you satisfied or not? Why do you have the situation you have, and what can you do to improve your situation? To change your results, you have to change your behavior.

Do you depend on your salary as your only income source? Bad luck. Your employment is out of your control, even if you are doing a good job. A lot of things can happen, financial crisis, cost reduction plans, relocations, etc., and your job is gone.

Does it have to be that way? No, it doesn't. However, you have to have the right attitude toward money to see the opportunities around you.

Do you want to be financially independent? Do you want to build your own money machine? Ask yourself what you wish your economy looks like in five years or in ten years from now. Imagine how it feels to have the stronger economy you aim for. Get inspired by what you see when you look at yourself in the future. Be motivated to take the first step in a new direction. Take one step, and then the next step. Keep moving in the right direction, and you will be there sooner than you think. Perhaps, you won't even notice it, because it would have become the new normal to you during this time.

You have to realize that you are in control of your destiny. You have to focus on building up your private economy, creating a positive cash flow every month, saving and investing regularly, and creating your own freedom in the future.

You must not depend solely on your income. People who accumulate a lot of wealth don't live off only on their salary, and they don't save pennies to get a lot of money. Although saving is a good habit, it should only be done for your retirement plans. The thing that will help you accumulate million dollars is an investment. Yes, investment is your golden ticket to a million dollar. It is by far the most trusted way of getting rich. However, don't take investment lightly. It requires a lot of research and experience. You must figure out which investment is the most beneficial. There are different types of investments, such as buying stocks, bonds, mutual funds, and certificates of deposits. The possibilities of investments are endless. Even if you start small investments in different places, you can gather a lot of money.

Every dollar is a seedling. Invest in your seedlings and watch them grow into a beautiful, lush, and vibrant tree that will stay with you for decades. Be smart and optimistic about your choices. Do not let other people decide where you should invest and when. There's nothing wrong with hiring a professional investor to help you with your journey. If anything, it is encouraged, especially if you haven't invested anywhere before. It is far better to ask for professional help. It will save you a lot of time, and you'll have to go through fewer stumbling blocks.

"When money realizes that it is in good hands, it wants to stay and multiply in those hands."

— Idowu Koyenikan,

Be smart about how you are spending your money. Money is something very hard to earn and very easy to spend. Before you know it, the hundred dollars you had in your account the other day disappears. It doesn't disappear, because you bought something for hundred dollars. It's usually the result of buying small items that we think we need but actually don't, like grabbing a cup of large coffee from the nearest Starbucks every day before going to work. You see something small you like, maybe a candle or pillows, even though you already have tons of them at home. The cost of inexpensive items accumulates, and by the end of the month, we wonder where our money went. We get shocked and can't believe what has happened. We say things like, "But I didn't even buy anything expensive." This is where smart saving comes into play. You need to be vigilant about where your money is going. Being a millionaire is not easy. You can't retain a million dollars if you keep spending it. This quote perfectly describes the point I'm making about being smart with money.

"The valuable prediction test on how you will spend $100 million dollars if you happen to win a lottery is to look at how you spent your last month's salary! With 100% precision, the two expenditures will have the same proportions."

— Dr. Lucas D. Shallua

Create a plan for saving every month. Set up an autosaving that the first day of your salary payout will transfer, for example, 10% or more of your monthly payouts to a safe harbor. The rest is for you and your monthly expenses. Still, save and invest at least 10% each month, and do it the first thing every month. If you wait to save until the end of the month, nothing will be left to save; that's how you are building a Money Machine, one that will grow stronger every month. Decrease your costs and increase your savings, and the Money Machine will grow faster.

You have to take control of your monthly cash flow. What you measure will be improved. You will never be rich with a high salary if you have the same level of costs or higher at the same time. It doesn't matter how high or low your salary is; you have to balance your costs and create an overbalance.

The best thing to help you to take control of your costs is to note your costs in a book or a similar tool. How much does your life cost each month? What do you really need, and what costs are unnecessary?

To get new results, you have to change something. How do you create bigger monthly savings? By reducing your expenses. The next is to compare your costs with your income. How big is your positive cash flow? Is it negative? Then, you have to take some action and reduce your expenses. If the cash flow is positive, how can it be increased?

When you have control over your expenses, the next thing is to look at your income. How can it be improved? By negotiating your current salary, getting a new and better-paying job, finding a side hustle, a hobby business, or anything.

The best is to do both, i.e., to decrease your expenses and increase your salary, to get a bigger gap and save more.

The next is to send the money to work for you. It's much better than you working for the money.

Another thing you must do to take control of your economy is to overcome any and every bad money habit. Remember being financially sound is the most powerful thing in the world. It is what helps us feel confident and deal with life's challenges a lot easier. If you are young, you may have experienced hardships because of our economy. You may have felt stuck at a certain point in your life and may want to accelerate your success and money-making abilities. In order for you to do that, you must know where your money is coming from and where it is going. Don't feel bad about not having a lot of money right now. This type of negativity will only hold you back from success. Instead, recognize them and work on them. Try to figure out why you don't have enough money in your bank account. What is it that you are doing? Are you spending too much on coffee? Or are you getting your food delivered every day? If you are doing one of the two, the solutions to break these habits are simple. First, start taking coffee from home to work. Second, start cooking at home. Cooking meals at home is cheaper and healthier. You won't pile up on all the calories and get satiated without wanting to get take out again.

"We are not to judge thrift solely by the test of saving or spending. If one spends what he should prudently save, that certainly is to be deplored. But if one saves what he should prudently spend, that is not necessarily to be commended. A wise balance between the two is the desired end." – Owen D. Young

Breaking bad habits is a process. Think about your life, money, savings and set a goal. Avoid living day-to-day. This is where most people lose out. They keep telling themselves it's okay if they spent more than they should have today because tomorrow is a new day. They keep using their credit cards without paying their previous month's bills and student loans or mortgages. These are all bad habits that need to be changed. The media has consistently convinced us that we need things in our life. We buy them and buy them and buy them until we have no money left. These are the things that we don't truly need.

Setting goals is how you take control of your life and money. When you set goals for how you will save money, everything will fall into place. The following quote describes the concept of saving money beautifully.

"Frugality is one of the most beautiful and joyful words in the English language, and yet one that we are culturally cut off from understanding and enjoying. The consumption society has made us feel that happiness lies in having things and has failed to teach us the happiness of not having things." – Elise Boulding

When you get control of your money, it makes you feel good. It makes you feel like you can control anything because saving is one of the most difficult tasks, especially in a society where hyper-consumerism is prevalent. When you see everybody around you spend money on things, it can be very difficult to hold yourself back from doing the same. But when you do, the results are amazing. Personal insight is also one of the reasons why people are able to control their money. They know what they require to live comfortably and when they are buying things they don't need.

Getting organized is a surefire way of saving money.

"Order is the sanity of the mind, the health of the body, the peace of the city, the security of the state. Like beams in a house or bones to a body, so is order to all things." - Robert Southey

Formulate a plan that will help you spend wisely. For example, make a list of grocery items you utilize every week and write down the price list. Calculate the end number and then try to eliminate items that you don't need. For example, cut fruit. It is cheaper to buy whole fruit. If there is something else that needs to be replaced with something cheaper, do so. Instead of taking an Uber, walk or take a bus. These things might seem small at first, but when they accumulate at the end of the year, the cost comes up to a lot. You'd be surprised by the end result.

A money machine is something that generates money for you 24/7, all day from early morning to late night, when you are sleeping, during the weekend, and when you are on a holiday. A Money Machine gives you financial freedom at some level, and it grows stronger over time.

But where can you put your money? You can invest wherever it creates a positive cash flow. It can be in a bank account that gives you an interest rate, the stock market, different kinds of commodities, your own business, an apartment house; it can be anything. Let your personal interest guide you to the way that's right for you.

Another excellent way of increasing your wealth is by buying stocks. A lot of people are scared of investing in stocks because of the volatility of the market, but the volatility is what makes profits. That is how the stock market is operated. If you are a beginner, the best way of investing in stocks is by putting money in an online investment account. It's an account used by beginners to buy mutual funds or stocks. A brokerage account is also used to invest in a single share. Here are a few ways you can invest in stocks.

The first thing you must do is choose the way you want to invest in stocks. You have to conduct a lot of research and then decide how you want to invest. If you want someone else to manage your investment, you can opt for a robo-advisor. Robo-advisor service offers low-cost investment options. It will outline different types of investments you can make. You can then decide where you'd like to invest depending on how much money you have.

The next step is to opt for an investing account. Typically, to invest, you should have an investment or a brokerage account. You can open a brokerage account online because it offers the cheapest and the quickest path of investing in stocks or funds. With the help of a broker, you can also open up IRA (individual retirement account). You might want to evaluate the brokers based on things like commissions, costs, fees, and so on. You should also thoroughly study the investment selection and what benefits you'll be getting long-term.

Understand the difference between the stocks. For example, there is a difference between stocks and mutual funds. Exchange-traded or stock mutual funds are funds that allow you to buy small but different stocks via a single transaction. When you invest in stock funds, you basically own small parts of different companies. When all those stocks are accumulated, they make up your portfolio. A good investor always ensures their portfolio is diverse. Stock mutual funds are also referred to as equity mutual funds.

On the other hand, individual stocks are different. You buy a specific company's stocks through a single transaction. You can either buy one share or multiple shares of one company. The best part about investing in stock mutual funds is the diversity that comes attached to it. It tends to lessen the risk involved in investing. Most beginners opt for stock mutual funds. According to Phil Town, an American investor and motivational speaker, "When it comes to investing, we want our money to grow with the highest rates of return, and the lowest risk possible. While there are no shortcuts to getting rich, there are smart ways to go about it."

In stock mutual funds, you don't get the returns immediately; however, you will get them for sure. When it comes to individual stocks, the chances of you being rich are extremely slim. It is nearly impossible to become a millionaire with individual stocks. You have to either wait for years for the market to go into a slum and then come up again or invest in stock mutual funds to see tangible results.

Ways to Increase Wealth

In regards to finances, you may be focused on a lot of different things. You may be too concerned about the numbers in the savings account, in your checking out, investing accounts, trading accounts, and retirement account, and so on. You could also be preoccupied with the amount you owe toward the mortgage, credit cards, or student loans. Tracking your income is a smart thing to do, especially when you are progressing in your career.

Keeping a check on all your accounts is important for understanding your financial health. However, the only thing that truly determines your financial future is net worth.

Net worth is the difference between the value of your assets such as retirement funds, house, checking account balance, investment accounts, and so on and the liabilities such as your credit card debt, mortgage, student loan, and more. It is an important piece of information to keep a check on when determining how much wealth you have and how much you owe. This should be determined before you retire, so you can live out your retirement comfortably.

Calculating your net worth is a simple process. Note down all your assets, including those in your retirement plan, as well as investments and stocks. Then, in a separate list, note down the outstanding balances such as credit card debts, and the amount you get after the difference between the two is your real net worth.

Take into Account Your Liability

One of the first steps is to find out the liability. As mentioned above, review your liabilities and reduce them or try to completely eliminate them if you can. Liabilities are what lands most people in trouble. It can take years to pay off loans. That's why it is recommended you try to ensure your liabilities don't increase in number after a certain point. In order to ensure you have plenty of wealth, you must have more assets compared to liabilities. The first step is to do everything in your power to pay off your debts, especially debts with the highest interest rates. That way, you'll get the big ones out of the way, and dealing with smaller debts will be easier.

Increase the Assets

Figure out your total assets and how they have changed over the years. This will allow you to understand whether your investments were fruitful or not. If your investments have reduced overtime and the assets have lost their value, this means you need to make better financial decisions. Or better yet, get a professional point of view by hiring an accountant. You must check how your rental properties are faring, how your state and stock investments are doing? What is the status of bonds, retirement, and mutual funds? Whether your assets are appreciating or depreciating, and if they are, by what percentage?

Here are some assets that are important.

Primary Residence

You have equity in your home. This is what you owe a mortgage on. You must have more equity in your house for your net worth to be higher.

Rental Property and Vacation Home

This is paid off with cash. This type of property is an essential asset. The equity also applies to this type of property.

Investments

Mutual funds, tax-deferred retirement plans, stocks, and bonds – all these will be added to your assets, but the tax paid on them will be in the liabilities category.

Collectibles

Fine vintage wines, classic cars, antiques, art, all these things are part of your assets. However, the prices of these items will fluctuate in the market. Therefore, you will need to determine their value before adding them to your asset's list.

When reviewing the assets and liabilities, ask yourself an important question about each of the items in the list. Find out ways you can increase your assets and lower your debt simultaneously.

Reduce Your Expenses

Millionaires don't become millionaires because they spend whatever money they have every day. They accumulate their wealth by reducing their expenses. It is easier said than done, but it is an excellent way to increase your net worth. Determine what your current expenses are and check if some of your expenditures can be cut back. Let's suppose you get coffee and a sandwich from Starbucks on your way to work. It may seem like a small amount, but over the span of one year, it can come up to a few hundred dollars, maybe even more. Try to eat out less and take lunch from home. You may be tempted to buy new clothes every time an event is taking place. Try to avoid doing that. Wherever you can, make sure you use the cash money you already have in your account instead of using your credit card and further adding to your credit card debt. People don't realize how much debt can be accumulated when they use a credit card. Sometimes it is so much that people can't pay off all of it in one lifetime. It is always best to be a bit frugal if you want to be a millionaire.

New Source of Income

Working 9 to 5 and occasionally investing in stocks is not going to cut it. If you want a lot of money under your belt, you will have to look for brand new sources of income. Finding new ways to earn money will not only help you pay off your debts but also increase your net worth. If you have some time and energy left, you can get a second job that can be part-time. Or the best way of earning a lot of money is to start your own business. If you happen to be great at baking, try your luck at selling baked goods or do some freelance jobs in digital marketing. If you are good at making paintings, sell them online. The possibilities are endless. If you want, you can do a lot. Make an Instagram or Facebook page. The age of social media has made it easier for people to start small businesses. If your business expands, you can quit your job focus on it fully to earn more money and hone your skills or stick to both working and handling business.

Increase Your Retirement Contributions

These contributions can help you in two ways. One way is that your taxable income is deferred because the contributions are taken off before taxes. Secondly, they help increase your assets. If the company you work for offers a retirement plan, immediately start contributing towards it. Retirement plans do much more than secure your future when you get old; they add to your assets. Also, open an IRA account and begin investing in it as soon as possible.

Storing Money Where it Grows

You'd think putting your money into saving accounts is a smart move. However, it is a misconception. Money doesn't grow in savings accounts, and the interest you get is very little. It is certainly not enough to land you the title of a millionaire. Store your money where it can grow exponentially, like investing in mutual funds. Even investing in a single stock is a long shot. You'll lose money before you even see it increase, which is a rare occasion. Long-term investment in mutual funds is the way to go. This method ensures guaranteed returns because there are other people involved. Also, make sure you don't experiment too much when it comes to investing; it might land you in hot waters. You may end up losing all your money and kiss your dreams and aspirations of becoming a millionaire goodbye.

Most people think it's scary to borrow money to buy stocks. However, they will gladly borrow money to buy a new car. Stocks are scary; you can lose money, and if you have borrowed money to buy the stocks, you are in trouble.

However, normally, the stock values will go up, and the car value will for sure go down.

When borrowing money to buy a car, you have to pay the interest rate and mortgage for the loan, and the car value will go down. If you borrow to buy stocks, the dividends from the stocks will pay your interest rates, and the stock values will normally go up.

If you use this method and let the time work for you, your stocks will give you the opportunity to pay the car with cash a few years later.

However, use the loan method carefully. If the stock market goes down, a borrowed stock portfolio shrinks faster than the one without any loans.

Choose the Right Type of Investment

The new beginner investor fails more often than the more experienced investor. It sounds quite obvious, right? But the consequence of that is that you will fail yourself to success! If you decide not to give up on some mistakes but instead learn from them. You will sooner or later be successful. Learn who you are as an investor. Analyze yourself with your pros and cons as an investor.

If you learn how to avoid big losses, the good deals will be in the majority. If you compare your results with an index, you must understand that an index is an average value based on results from a selection of companies. If you avoid the worst-performing companies, you will automatically perform better than the index. If you use the time and keep performing over the index, your portfolio will increase exponentially over time using the compounding effect.

Choosing where to invest is a crucial thing when it comes to accumulating wealth.

Courage

If you have a dream, it will remain a dream until you act. Sometimes, it is scary to do something new, and you need to find the courage to act. However, if you never act, nothing will happen. Bravery is a rare quality these days. It takes a brave soul to step out of their comfort zone and aim for what they desire. If you have a dream, you must do everything you can to achieve it. There is no point in sitting in your living room and thinking about it day in and day out. If you want to become rich, become a millionaire, then do your research, read up on what you can do to achieve your goal.

Start saving up if you have to; if there are a few vacations you have to miss to save money, do it. Saving money and becoming a millionaire is not easy. It takes courage and perseverance to reach that point. If you read or watch any millionaire's interview, they will talk about all the hardships they had to go through to get where they are. They will talk about how everyone around them tried to stop them or discourage them from doing what they wanted, but it was courage that helped them fulfill their dreams.

"Before you can become a millionaire, you must learn to think like one. You must learn how to motivate yourself to counter fear with courage." —Thomas J. Stanley

The above quote sums it up perfectly. Strategize your moves before taking a step, but take it nonetheless. Become the force to be reckoned with. Your drive to become a millionaire should help you lead the path you want in your life to make it happen.

Desire

There is a difference between hope, wish, and desire. Desire comes from an obsession. In your mind, you are already there. You can see yourself in the future at a specific place, a specific position, or similar. It is something definite. You can't compromise with yourself. All you want is to realize your dream.

Faith

To reach your dream, your target, you must believe in it. You must have faith, and faith is a state in your mind in which you know you will make it.

Both financial freedom and poverty are a result of your thoughts.

Imagination

Use your imagination to create a plan. You can create almost anything you can imagine. Everything you can see around you has started as an idea in someone's mind.

What would your lifestyle look like if you had an unlimited amount of money? Do you realize that you can do both and that they are not necessarily linked to each other? You can do your best to build up your financial wealth. However, you can also move in the direction of the lifestyle you dream of without having unlimited money. However, sometimes, you have to think outside the box to see the opportunities around you.

Just move step-by-step in that direction and remember that man normally overestimates what he can achieve in one year while underestimating what he can achieve in ten years at the same time.

Decision

After Decision comes Action, and that's where things start happening. Time is the next to go, from Decision to Action and Speed, make things happen now, not later, and move in the right direction. It doesn't need to move fast, but don't wait to do it. Don't change your decision repeatedly. The purpose is to move in one specific direction. If you change your decision and target, you will also lose time and momentum.

The combination of desire and willpower or persistence is important for being able to follow your plan and reach your objectives.

When you create your Big Target and can see yourself in the future, you will also be able to divide your major plan into sub-targets. Set sub-targets and make sure they all move in the direction of the major target. Celebrate when you have reached each sub-target because then, you know it's just a matter of time until you reach your Big Target as long as you keep reaching the sub-targets one by one. When you have reached the Big Target, you will also have the Reward; you will live the lifestyle you wish to have.

Why the First Million Is the Hardest to Attain?

Some people say that attaining your first million dollars is the hardest. Having a lot of money already makes it easier to earn more, but hitting a million-dollar milestone is not as easy. We have been told that the American dream is to have equal opportunity to make money and get rich by hard work and drive. Many people have succeeded, but some have failed or given up in the middle of their journey.

Once you hit the one million mark, it is easier to increase your wealth. You know, it's said, "Money makes more money." It's the reason for rich people getting richer. If you accumulate one million dollars, you often don't even need to work extra hard to make another million. Making different smart investments is the best way to make more. Considering the economy is not in the slump. The more risk you take when it comes to investments, the higher the stakes, and that's why it's so hard to make your first million dollars.

Here are some other reasons why it's so hard to make your first million.

Psychological

The first reason why most people can't make their first million is fear. It is what blocks most people. Their fear of not being able to make it is very real. Million dollars is a lot of money, and with it, comes a lot of fear. People have doubts and lack of belief which hinders them from doing everything they can to accumulate that much wealth. However, once they have attained million dollars, it gives them the confidence to make more. They feel like they have achieved something tremendous, and it motivates them to work harder and multiply their money.

People are no longer hesitant because any psychological strain or interference disappears.

Toughness

Every win leads to the next one. Emotional and mental strengths are the most important aspects of success after hard work and motivation. Accumulating the first million forges a new reality for people. Think about a famous musician or an actor; they know that after their first or second successful gig, they don't have to lift a finger to make their ends meet. They don't even have to act or sing; they invest in other businesses such as fashion, restaurants, real estate, and so on.

After one is successful, they get motivated to do more. Contrary to popular belief, money is the main motivator for most people. Only a few people don't care much about making millions, and most of us work 9 to 5 to secure our future. When you get your first million, it raises your consciousness. They see endless possibilities, and suddenly, everything seems attainable. Money becomes your weapon, your tool. All you need to do is get out of your way. Don't get scared.

After attaining your first million, you feel like you can make all your dreams come true. You feel like anything, and everything is possible. This emotional power allows you to move forward. The success of getting the first million dollars separates you from the critics, skeptics, and nay-sayers.

Confidence

Once you have earned your million dollars, your confidence increases ten-fold. You are more sure of yourself and calm. You become certain that once you have secured the million, you can do it again. The confidence you get helps you focus on your next challenge. Most of the time, it is no one but yourself who stands in the way of your fortune. Once you get out of your way, you begin believing that you can do anything.

Mistakes People Make With Their First Million

The more money you have, the harder it is to maintain it and keep it balanced. Accumulating the first million is hard, but not losing it all in a short period is harder. That is why you should have a long-term financial plan.

When people receive a large amount of money, they already mentally plan how they will spend it. There is a reason why lottery winners can't retain their money. They tend to file for bankruptcy a couple of years after winning the lottery.

It is not how much you make. What matters is how much you can save. The common problem with those who never achieve financial success is not having a proper financial plan.

Here are a few mistakes you can avoid after getting your first million.

Not Keep Up with the Joneses

Life is not a competition; so, don't treat it like one. Everybody has their own journey, their own path to follow. Therefore, you can't compare your lifestyle to someone else's. Treating your efforts to build your wealth like a competition is not good for you or your self-esteem. It can be tempting to compare your lifestyle with others, but you need to understand that you may not be living the same way as others. If someone can spend thousands of dollars on jewelry or cars doesn't mean you can do the same. Be smart about how you handle your money.

You don't truly know other people's financial situation. Maybe they can afford to spend a lot of money because of a lucrative investment you don't know about, or they have an inheritance. OR maybe, they can't afford anything and are drowning in debt.

Ask yourself what is important to you. Is it showing your wealth or growing it? Financial growth should be your top priority. Once you have secured money for your future and made plenty of smart investments, you can spend freely. Until then, you must be frugal. You should base your financial decisions on your financial situation, not anyone else's.

Not Thinking About the Next Step

Another common mistake people make after getting their first million dollars is not having a proper financial plan. Attaining your very first million dollars may make you feel invincible. However, there won't be million dollars sitting in your bank account if you don't have any plans to make another million dollars. If you sit idly and spend all of it, or wait for it to grow, it will never grow. You will watch your money dwindle away.

Once you have accumulated all the money, you should think about your legacy. It is your responsibility to retain it and plan for the future. Start by noting down everything important to you and all your financial goals. Envision yourself after five or ten years. Think about where you want to see yourself in the future and how your financial plans will work with your goals. Think about these questions and then work on finding their answers. Make a list according to your priorities. One list should be all your short-term goals, and another should consist of your long-term goals.

These are the things you should have on your list.

- The first action step should be the target dates. This step is important because you will get a clear vision of what you want from life.
- Set reminders of your goals.
- You should also include business goals, personal development, family goals, and lifestyle goals. First, achieve the goal most important to you, and then

move on to the next. Keep reviewing your list from time to time to determine where you stand.

No Protection

Don't be greedy. You must understand that the more money you attain, the riskier your investments might become. Most people become way too comfortable taking risky steps to make more money and end up losing it all. The higher risk may give you higher returns, but that is never a guaranteed thing. Be smart about your investments.

As soon as you get your first million, work on protecting it. Many people either get too busy wanting to spend their money or making risky investments, but they forget to protect it. Protect your money by getting insurance. If something happens and you don't have insurance, you will find yourself in a tough spot. It is going to be very difficult for you to financially recover.

Determine the type of risks you might encounter and get insurance. Also, work on protecting your loved ones. The risks most people commonly encounter are the loss of income, having an accident, and developing health issues.

You can get insurance for your health; you can get homeowners insurance, automobile, disability, or professional liability insurance. There are many options available out there.

Also, think about what is required by looking at your financial situation. Do your research and learn about different types of insurance. Make an informed decision and protect yourself and your loved ones.

Another excellent way to protect your wealth is by coming up with an investment plan. You should have cash reserves that ensure your money is constantly circulating, whether in bonds, stocks, or real estate. Diversify your portfolio to spread the risk. Never invest all your money in a single stock. If you don't want to invest in many companies or take that much risk, slow down your investments. But know that if you invest less money, your returns will also be smaller. If you want higher rewards, then the risk attached will also be higher.

A smart investor analyzes the risks and then balances the risk and rewards both. Having a diverse portfolio is the key to success. It is what will keep you wealthy for a long time.

Before spending money, think about saving. Always pay your debt first, or Plan on paying for yourself. Paying for yourself means you should have a good financial strategy in place before you go out and start spending your money. It doesn't mean you don't spend any money at all. Just have a solid financial plan.

Saving money is not as difficult as most people think. It is a simple set-up. All you need to do is choose an option so that a fixed amount automatically gets deducted from your account and gets added to your savings account. You can also get an amount deducted from your payroll and into your retirement account. Bank transfers can also be set up to save money.

You have to make an effort to save money, especially if you plan on saving an amount aside for the long term.

Putting some money aside as savings is better, that way you can be more comfortable taking risks. You will also have enough to pay for basic day-to-day expenses after you retire.

Your current financial situation will determine how much money you should save and when you should start saving. Preferably, one should start saving money soon after getting a job. Ultimately, how much money you have saved up matters the most. The last thing you want is to be dependent on your cash flow. Because once you retire, there will be no cash flow. Make saving money a habit.

Not Enough Diversification

Another huge mistake people make with their money is not diversify their investments. They put all their eggs in one basket. Different investments react differently to market conditions. Therefore, a diverse portfolio acts as a cushion against the market slumps, ensuring you don't lose all your money. If one asset takes a hit, you always have other assets or investments to rely on. Diversification helps reduce the risk. There is no single formula to ensure you get high returns from your investments. You just need to invest wisely. Try to diversify your assets by dividing them into the categories below:

- Business interests
- Bonds and stocks, including ETFs and mutual funds

- Real estate assets such as income property, vacation home, or primary residence
- Alternative assets
- Cash reserves

Take your financial needs into account and diversify accordingly. Make sure the investments you make are aligned with your financial goals. Also, consider working with a professional or an accountant to help you with your portfolio.

When it comes to accumulating wealth, there is no guarantee of how much you can gather. The best thing to do is do plenty of research and develop a solid financial plan to help you make smart decisions aligned with your long-term goals. You will make mistakes, there will be times where you might lose some money, but if you do your best and are smart about handling money, you'd be able to recover quickly.

Doing all of the above will help you multiply your first million dollars into a lot more money than you can imagine. All it takes is a little bit of discipline and a lot of smart planning.

Where to Invest Your First Million Dollars

If someone gave you a million dollars and asked you to return the money double the amount in five years, you'd probably refuse. It is because you may not be aware of how a million dollars can multiply if you were to play your cards right. Most people find doubling the money they have very hard, especially if the amount is as big as a million dollars.

Now that you have a million dollars in your bank account, you must learn how to multiply them. Before planning on increasing your wealth, there are a few questions you must ask yourself.

The first question should be regarding your financial goals. Create an investment plan and figure out what your personal goals are. Once you have a clear direction, you can ask yourself the second question. The second question is related to your timeline. When do you plan on achieving your goals? How long will you give yourself for achieving the first few steps or the short-term goals?

If you want to save up for retirement, you should look for long-term goals. If you think you will be required to access your investment money, opt for a short-term strategy.

The third question to ask yourself would be related to your risk tolerance. If you are not that concerned with losing your investment, it means you have more than one income stream or have a lot of money saved up, increasing your risk tolerance.

Lending

The first most effective way of investing your million dollars is by private lending. For instance, if you borrow money from someone and then lend it to someone else. That is how the banks work. They borrow funds from the Fed and then add a 3 percent mark and then lend it to the people.

If you are to borrow one million dollars for the next five years and add a six percent interest and then lent it to someone else at a nine percent interest, you would be earning approximately $30,000 every year and $150,000 over five years.

The trick is to lend money to someone you trust and someone who you know will return it. If there is a possibility of them not paying back then it is best to set up an agreement with collateral. Most collateral is some property, like a house. Collateral must cost as much if not more than the money owed and that includes sales costs.

Real Estate

Another best investment you can make with your first million dollars is in real estate. If you invest in properties at the right market and at the right time, you can easily grow your wealth to millions of dollars. You'd also be able to get a nine percent return per year.

For example, you purchased around ten properties, each costing $100,000. You rent them out for $1000 per month. You will get the same amount earned by being a private lender above. The only difference is that you'd have closing costs of about $3000. You'd be making $120,000 after five years.

If the cost of the homes is appreciated three percent every year, then you can make an additional $150,000. You could sell eight of those properties, which could help you pay back your loans and debts, and keep the remaining two. With those remaining two you'd be getting a cash flow and won't have to worry about the mortgage. You'd also be left with some money in your pocket, which you can invest in other areas to make more cash.

On the other hand, if the value of homes gets appreciated by four percent, then you'd only have to sell seven of your properties to help pay back your loans and keep the remaining homes. If the value goes up by six percent, which is not unlikely. You'd be minting money. The return on investment when it comes to real estate is impressive. If you want to multiply your million dollars, this is the way to go.

Business

There is also an option of taking your million dollars and investing them in a successful business idea. These days a lot of people have been going down the path of opening up their business instead of working 9 to 5. It is a great way to make quick money if the business plan is successful. If everything works out you can double your investment.

However, launching your business comes with several risks because statistically, almost 50% of businesses fail in the first five years. Then the entrepreneurs are left with enormous debts. That is why banks are skeptical to give loans to people wanting to launch their business venture.

Even you have an excellent credit history and an amazing idea, banks are still on the fence about it. Because if the business fails, you'd be left with an enormous debt, that you might not be able to pay back to the bank. Then your house would be the collateral rendering you homeless.

This is why you must think a hundred times before wanting to launch your own business. Even if your family or friends come to you for help and ask you to invest in their business, you must think about it before taking this step. Even if their business idea is impressive. If they offer no collateral you might not get your money back because at the end of the day we must think about the worst-case scenarios. This is the type of risk that should be left to venture capital firms because they can afford to incur such losses.

Banks on the other hand prefer lending money on properties, not so much on businesses. They want to know if the property is worth much more than the money they lend you, whether you can afford to pay part of the amount back every month and that the amount of money you have borrowed is something you can handle. You shouldn't take up more debt after borrowing from the banks.

If you are someone who can pay their bills on time and have a great credit history, the bank will offer you the best rate possible. However, even if you don't have a good credit history, you will still get the loan. The Federal Housing Administration doesn't see the risk of giving a loan to someone with a foreclosure two years before asking for the loan. If you can't pay it back, they will simply take over the property.

Mitchell Bloom of Bloom Financial, LLC states that if someone is an accredited investor and is not afraid of a bit of risk, then they should consider investing in businesses as an angel investor.

An angel investor is someone who is usually interested in funding start-up companies and can invest between $10,000 to $100,000 on each project. However, as mentioned earlier, if the business fails, you lose all the money. Remember Theranos? The company that had the potential to make its angel investors very rich, at least that's what they assumed when the business idea was first laid out on the table. The business not only failed but became the most controversial business venture out there.

If you are considering becoming an angel investor, you must have enough money on the side just for this, because if the company fails, you will still have more money to support yourself and invest somewhere else.

It is also recommended you conduct thorough research into the business you want to invest in. Do not rush into investing and don't invest because you feel like you will miss out on the opportunity of a lifetime. In other words, don't be greedy. There are hundreds of start-up companies being launched every day and not a single one guarantees a 100% success rate.

Mitchell Bloom says "There are Angel investor groups all over the country and the largest is called the Keiretsu Forum, based out of California. If approved for membership, you can gain access to a wide array of opportunities."

Businesses on this platform are vetted thoroughly by a committee and there is a formal process to ensure no fraud takes place.

Stock Market

This is a no-brainer. The first thing anyone wants to do after they receive a lot of money is to invest in a stock market. Investing money in a stock market can give you a lot of money in return, provided you invest smartly and don't be too greedy.

Warren Buffet once said that greed and fear are diseases that infect investors. He stated "Occasional outbreaks of those two super-contagious diseases fear and greed will forever occur in the investment community. The timing of these epidemics will be unpredictable. And the market aberrations produced by them will be equally unpredictable, both as to duration and degree."

He continued, "Therefore, we never try to anticipate the arrival or departure of either disease. Our goal is more modest: We simply attempt to be fearful when others are greedy and to be greedy only when others are fearful."

The stock market is volatile and susceptible to ups and downs. It can go through both small and large fluctuations. While people see big returns, there are huge losses too. If you are considering investing your million dollars in the stock market, understand that it will be risky.

You cannot make money if there is no risk involved. According to Peter Lynch "You get recessions, you have stock market declines. If you don't understand that's going to happen, you're not ready, you won't do well in the markets."

Remember to spread your risk thin by investing in different places. Diversify your portfolio to minimize the risk.

Real Estate Investment Trusts or REITs

Real estate investment trusts are becoming popular day by day. These trusts allow you to invest in real estate without having to purchase a property. Instead, you can buy bigger projects and own equity as a whole. This is an excellent way of stepping into the domain of real estate without having to take out a lot of cash.

Super Saver Accounts

Whether you make use of a robo-advisor, a professional financial advisor, or manage your investments by yourself, Super Saver Accounts is a great service offered by several financial companies. Betterment an American financial advisory company offers an account called "Smart Saver". It moves the excess cash into a low-risk bond. This way, you can receive higher returns with a regular savings account. Robo-advisor accounts earn 2.23% APY.

Wealthfront, an investment firm from California, U.S. also works with cash management with a return of 2.24% APY.

Annuities

This is another way of investing your million dollars. It is a reasonable option that can increase your wealth outside of the stock market. There are different types of annuities you can buy, these include variable annuities. You should never purchase a variable annuity.

It is important to remember that when you buy annuities, you make a contract with an insurance company. In return for a lump of cash and you usually get paid every month. A fixed annuity promises you a specific payment each month. On the other hand, a variable annuity pays you depending on how the investment performs. There is a fixed-indexed annuity, which is a combination of both a fixed-rate and variable annuity. It offers higher returns and lesser risk overall.

Conclusion

Earning your first million dollars is tough but once you achieve that milestone, it is the greatest feeling in the world. It can be tempting to spend it all on everything you have ever wanted in your life. However, saving it and multiplying it is worthwhile. It helps you build your legacy and secure your future as well as that of your loved ones.

Millionaires like Mark Zuckerberg and Jeff Bezos have their financial status for a reason. The difference between us and them is that they focus on their personal growth and have an unparalleled drive. They plan everything and work on their wealth-building strategies. Every day, they wake up wanting to do better. They also talk about how much support they had from their family members and friends.

Jeff Bezos said, "If you don't get that kind of support somehow – it doesn't have to be your parents, sometimes people get lucky and it's the grandparent, or a friend, or a family friend, or a teacher. But you need that. Somebody has to step into your life."

Mark Zuckerberg gave a speech at Harvard University. In this speech, he said, "The greatest successes come from having the freedom to fail." He further added, "If ... I didn't know I'd be fine if Facebook didn't work out, I wouldn't be standing here today."

There is a bit of luck, support, hard work, and discipline involved in being successful and attaining a vast amount of wealth. It is not as easy as it looks, but it's also not impossible.

"Financial peace isn't the acquisition of stuff. It's learning to live on less than you make, so you can give money back and have money to invest. You can't win until you do this."
— Dave Ramsey